Am I
GREAT
at Customer Service?

*25 Characteristics
of People Great at*
Customer Service

ED GAGNON

Copyright © 2010 Ed Gagnon
All rights reserved.

ISBN: 1452845018
ISBN-13: 9781452845012
Library of Congress Control Number: 2010906359

Dedication

This book is dedicated to my parents, Donald and Eleanor Gagnon, who have always provided me with love and support of my decisions through my education, marriage, work, and life in general.

I also want to recognize my wife, Alicia, for her ongoing support of what I do, continuous faith in the guiding principles of my work, and belief in the value of customer service. She's a wonderful friend, coach, supporter, and example of what it means to be a great person.

Contents

Dedication	iii
Introduction	vii
CSS Background	ix
Is Your Attitude Great?	1
How full is the cup?	1
What's the balance in your knowledge bank?	11
Patience…patience…	15
Set aside the status quo.	19
Focus like a laser.	25
Do you realize they're all individuals?	29
Do you know everything already?	33
Meet the co-workers.	37
Do you fear confrontation?	41
Calculate Your Greatness – Is Your Attitude Great?	46
Are You Great When You're In Front of the Customer?	49
Think before you speak?	53
Your actions speak so loudly that…	57
Here comes a call!	63
Listen up!	69
They're angry. What are you going to do?	73
I want to be King of the World!	79

Calculate Your Greatness –
    Are You Great When You're In Front of the Customer? 84

Are You Great When the Customer's Not in Front of You? 87
    Find the common ground.   *91*
    To be or not to be…in touch.   *97*
    Don't drop the ball.   *101*
    Do you waste your own time?   *107*
    I need a quick response.   *113*
    Do it right the first time.   *117*
    Your fault?   *123*
    Are you a Mr. (or Ms.) Fix-it?   *129*
    You don't have to be Shakespeare, but…   *133*
    Why are we here?   *139*

Calculate Your Greatness –
    Are You Great When the Customer's
    Not in Front of You? 144

Calculate Your Greatness – Overall 150

Remember that People Great at Customer Service… 151

About the Author 153

Introduction

Are you great at customer service?

I don't mean good or above average. I don't mean *"Are you nice?"* or *"Do you have a warm smile?"* I mean, are you GREAT at customer service?

If you are reading this book, maybe it is because you want to be great. Maybe it's because you think you are, or you're getting very close. Maybe you were given this book because somebody wants you to be great. Or, just maybe, you just care about continuously trying to learn how to get better.

Whatever your reason for reading this, it's important to have an understanding of what this book is intended to do. It's intended to paint a picture of some of the most important characteristics that people demonstrate who want to be great at customer service.

So much of the world today, particularly in America, is driven by service industries. Even if you are in a manufacturing industry, there are so many functions that require you to serve others, serve clients, serve internal customers, and even serve vendors and suppliers.

So this can apply to virtually anybody who – as part of their role – needs to serve and satisfy others.

The key characteristics discussed in this book have been determined by Customer Service Solutions, Inc. co-founder Ed Gagnon based on his 20+ years of work in the world of customer service. If you become highly effective at living these principles, taking on these traits, and continuously trying to do better in building your attitude and skills, then you will be taking a dynamic step toward reaching the very top level of the occupation you undertake.

We give you guidelines on what these important characteristics are, we tell you stories to illustrate what it looks like when these characteristics are lived as well as when these characteristics are ignored. And we give you a series of self-tests so that you can evaluate yourself and determine "Am I Great at...Customer Service?"

In the television show "So You Think You Can Dance," thousands of people audition for the show thinking they're great dancers. But many are REALLY wrong about this self-assessment!

We've conducted customer service training sessions where participants (especially early on in the session) say "I know all about customer service...why do I keep having to come back to these courses?" Usually, it becomes readily apparent during the session that these folks don't exactly have service attitudes or the best skills out there, even though they think they're great.

But there are truly some outstanding customer service-oriented people in this world. Do you think you're one of them?

It's fine to think you're great at customer service. Confidence is an important part of service success. But we need to understand what it takes to be on the road to greatness. We'll provide you with 100 questions to consider and 25 key qualities to strive to develop.

We hope this book helps you to learn, to grow, and to become great!

CSS Background

Customer Service Solutions, Inc. is a management consulting firm focused entirely on customer service and client retention. CSS has conducted research and provided consulting and training services since 1998. This book has been crafted from the thousands and thousands of mystery shopping experiences (where we and our shoppers pose as customers to evaluate telephone, e-mail, onsite, and website experiences for our clients). The characteristics were defined through the observations of those who are great (and those not so great) in the world of customer service.

The skills are taken directly from much of the training content that we provide to clients, where we guide them in how to improve communications with, relationships with, and satisfaction from their customers. We have conducted hundreds of projects, trained thousands of individuals on many of the principles and skills noted in this book. Now we are using all our experience and expertise to provide this core set of key characteristics for anyone wanting to be great at customer service.

Enjoy learning about customer service.

We want you to be GREAT!

Is Your Attitude Great?

People who are great at customer service are typically more upbeat, hopeful, focused more on what <u>can</u> be done instead of what <u>can't</u> be done. Is that you?

You need to have the attitude that drives success. That's an attitude of "yes we can," of "I hope so," of "it's got a better chance to be a great day if I try to make it a great day."

How full is the cup?

People Great at Customer Service…
Have a Positive Orientation

What is your mindset on a typical day? Is it a mindset of what can be done or what can't be done? Individuals who are great at customer service have a mindset of *"how can I help a customer achieve their goal, how can I address their needs, how can I say 'yes' to what will accomplish that goal even if I have to say 'no' to the particular solution or method or timeframe that they desire?"*

People who are negative seem to ooze negativity; it's like an odor that permeates their being and impacts both customers and co-workers alike. Sure they may smile and tell jokes occasionally, but there's a certain air about them that dampens the laughter and questions the sincerity of the smile. There's an orientation of *"No"* or *"We've already tried that"* or *"That won't work."*

Your attitude and orientation are choices. Maybe they're learned behaviors, but they are habits that can change for people who are wired more negatively.

People who are great at customer service are inherently more positive.

Illustrating the point...
It was a simple little exercise, but it made the impression of a lifetime. The social studies teacher told his freshman high school class to take an index card, and he asked each student to write their name at the top. So Rickie put his name at the top of the card. Then the teacher said to start passing the cards

up and down the rows until everyone had written one positive thing about the person whose name was on the card.

After the exercise was done, Rickie and his classmates got their own cards back, and Rickie began to read. It was great to read the positive things his classmates said about him. But of all the comments, one stuck out. One classmate wrote "Never a bad word about anybody." Rickie sat and smiled; it was nice that somebody would notice and appreciate that about him. Rickie took the initials of each word that made up that statement and was proud to be a NABWAA. It was his way to remember a characteristic that he didn't want to change.

But as Rickie became Rick the adult, it became harder and harder to be a NABWAA. There were lots of people he worked with who complained about co-workers or about customers. They'd gripe about management or about some vendor. It was a way to socialize and bond – one person says something negative about someone else, and they both agree.

Maybe this was part of being an adult in the workforce. After all, people need to vent their frustrations sometimes.

But some people took it too far. It seemed like ALL they did was talk negatively about others. It was like it was their quest to put others down. Rick wasn't sure if the reason for all the negativity was to vent or for folks to build themselves up by badmouthing the others. Rick began to realize that, for these people, there was never a GOOD word about anybody. They were NAGWAAs.

The more he spent time with them, the more he found himself bad-mouthing co-workers and customers, the less fun work was, and the more negative he got in general.

You see, NAGWAAs are often self-centered. When an issue arises, what's important is who's to blame (as long as it's not them). When asked for help, they focus on what cannot be done. When they're uncertain, they focus on the likelihood of failure instead of the possibility of success.

The NAGWAAs were like a corporate cancer bringing negativity into his work life and having that filter into his mindset at home.

Don't be a NAGWAA.

Rate Yourself

Rate Your Level of Agreement:
3 = Strongly Agree, 2 = Agree, 1 = Do Not Agree

1. I clearly communicate to the customer or co-worker that I want to help them.
   Rating: _____

2. I am more focused on resolving the issue than determining who is to blame.
   Rating: _____

3. I am more focused on conveying to the customer or co-worker what I can do or what they can do rather than what I cannot or they cannot do.
   Rating: _____

4. I try to convey realistic hope to the customer or co-worker instead of consistent doubt.
   Rating: _____

Total Chapter Score: _____

Record your Total Score in the "Calculate Your Greatness" table at the end of this Section.

Questions to Consider – Write Responses Below

Do you try to see the positive side of circumstances?

Do people sense that you care about them and their needs?

Do you help to create an upbeat, realistic but hopeful, and positive environment with co-workers and customers?

How can you create a more positive mindset?

What's the balance in your knowledge bank?

People Great at Customer Service…
Hone Their Knowledge/Skills

People who are great at customer service have the knowledge and skills to be successful. They realize that attitude is only a piece of the puzzle. In customer service, an employee's knowledge can be placed into three different categories:

- **Knowledge of Your Customer**. An individual employee's knowledge of his or her customers stems from an inquisitive nature. Ask yourself: Do I try to gather information on my customers? Do I ask customers questions to determine who they are, what their situations are, and what they truly need?

- **Knowledge of Your Products and Services**. This is where the best employees, those who are great at customer service, have such a great wealth of knowledge of the products and services their organization has to offer that they have a greater set of alternatives from which to choose. They are therefore more able to meet an individual customer's needs and goals.

- **Knowledge of Your Policies and Procedures**. The more knowledgeable you are, both in terms of how things are done and what can and cannot be done, the more creative you can be in addressing customers' needs and issues.

Illustrating the point...

One of my favorite sports/business quotes is from Vince Lombardi, former Head Coach of the Green Bay Packers. He stated that "A man who is trained to his peak capacity will gain confidence. Confidence is contagious and so is lack of confidence, and a customer will recognize both."

What Lombardi advocates is for individuals to have and convey confidence in their capabilities, in their company, in their job, in their product, in their services. Customers notice confidence, and they are attracted to and made confident by confident employees. So if employees want to be confident, how do they do that?

First, know your customer. The better you know your customer, the more confident you can be that you're suggesting the right solution to their problem. Next, know your product/service. The more knowledgeable you are of what you offer, the better you can speak to the benefits of and appropriate application of that product. Also, know your policies and procedures. If you know HOW your services are delivered, you'll instill confidence in the mind of the customer that the fulfillment process will work to their liking.

To help the customer feel confident in you and your service, know your customers, your products/services, and your policies and procedures.

Rate Yourself

Rate Your Level of Agreement:
3 = Strongly Agree, 2 = Agree, 1 = Do Not Agree

1. I know my customers very well, or I ask questions to get to know them well.
   Rating: _____

2. I am very knowledgeable about our company's policies and procedures.
   Rating: _____

3. I am very knowledgeable about our product and service offerings.
   Rating: _____

4. I am very good at applying the appropriate policy, procedure, product, and/or service to the situation based on the customer and their needs.
   Rating: _____

Total Chapter Score: _____

Record your Total Score in the "Calculate Your Greatness" table at the end of this Section.

Questions to Consider — Write Responses Below

Do you ask enough appropriate questions of the other person, and then listen to their answers?

Do you try to learn more about your products and services, your policies, and procedures?

Do you put all that knowledge to use?

How could you improve your knowledge base?

Patience...patience...

People Great at Customer Service...
Convey Patience

Are you patient with the customer or are you trying to end the conversation as quickly as possible? To the customer, impatience conveys indifference. And there is no more effective way to break a relationship than to convey that you are indifferent or do not care about the customer.

Individuals who are great at customer service understand the need to convey patience and how to do so.

Illustrating the point...
Jay wanted to order his wife a new gas grill for her anniversary. He visited a website and found one he liked. It had a side unit to warm a pot, two racks for cooking, a storage area underneath, and – to top it off – a built-in bottle opener! For his wife, of course.

He selected the silver model, and – as he attempted to place the order – the system kept kicking him out when he was on the order screen. Again and again, he had to reselect the unit and re-key his credit card information, only to have the system kick him out again.

Frustrated, Jay called the toll-free customer service number. When the representative got on the phone, Jay calmly began to explain his issue. As soon as he mentioned the credit card screen, the representative interrupted and said, "You need to fill in all the required fields."

Jay responded, "I did. The system didn't notify me that there were any incomplete fields."

He was interrupted again. "You need to enter that security code on the back of your credit card or it won't work."

Jay responded, "I did; I entered the name and number and code 3 times, and then…"

The representative interrupted once again, saying, "You need to…"

"Now hold it," Jay responded. "Don't interrupt me! You need to listen to me, and you can't listen if you're talking! Let me tell you what happened, and quit blaming me."

There was a pause in the conversation.

Jay went on to describe in detail what happened. This time around, the representative asked Jay to walk through the issue online while he was on the phone. It turned out that the company was out of the silver version of the grill, causing the system to give an error every time Jay tried to order because of this.

So the next time there's a customer issue, don't hear one key word and assume you know the answer. Don't interrupt, and don't blame the customer. Don't be the cause of the confrontation.

Be patient.

Rate Yourself

Rate Your Level of Agreement:
3 = Strongly Agree, 2 = Agree, 1 = Do Not Agree

1. I am very patient with customers when they are asking a question, making a request, or conveying information.
   Rating: _____

2. I avoid interrupting the customer if at all possible.
   Rating: _____

3. I convey my patience with relaxed body language, expressions, and a tone of voice that convey interest.
   Rating: _____

4. I firmly believe it is necessary to understand the customer's situation prior to taking action.
   Rating: _____

Total Chapter Score: _____

Record your Total Score in the "Calculate Your Greatness" table at the end of this Section.

Questions to Consider – Write Responses Below

Do you convey patience to the other person?

Do you have the ability to work quickly without unnecessarily rushing others?

How can you get better at conveying patience?

Set aside the status quo.

People Great at Customer Service…
Have a Kaizen Mindset

Please realize that you shouldn't have to deal with the same complaints and issues over and over again. Try to find the root causes of problems. Realize a lot of little improvements are great; focus on tapping into co-workers, staff, and customers for ideas. Always try to do things better.

Kaizen is a management philosophy with several permutations which have evolved from it over the years. The definition I like best is that *Kaizen* literally means "Change Good." In other words, it's not change for the sake of change. It's changing to improve. One way you can apply this term is to evaluate your own work on an ongoing basis to identify and implement small incremental improvements in your day-to-day job.

Imagine every employee in your organization making one or two changes each week. Whether that means automating some manual step, eliminating old records, relocating machines so there is less walking required, or reorganizing soft and hard copy files to more quickly find information, that would add up to a tremendous amount of "Change Good" in any organization over the course of a year.

If you're great at customer service, you're probably better than you were a month ago, better than a year ago. You've improved. And as with anything else in business, if you're not moving ahead, then you're falling behind.

Illustrating the point...
As customer service consultants, we spend a lot of our time talking about continuous improvement; we're always trying to figure out how to be better. The reason why this desire for improvement is so important is that competition, technological advances, and other business innovations are all factors you cannot control, but which can dramatically influence your organization's relative success or failure. The level of your future success often is dependent on your company becoming better tomorrow than it is today.

Noted below are several questions that your department or organization should ask itself. Take these questions to a department meeting or leadership gathering, and use them to create dialogue and promote creative ways to improve:

- If our department (or company) didn't exist, how would that negatively impact the customer? How can we expand our positive impact on the customer?
- What are two things that we do now that we could really stop doing?
- What are two of the biggest causes of customer complaints? What could we do to eliminate the root causes of the complaints such that we wouldn't hear these same complaints anymore?
- What is the biggest barrier to success in this organization? How do we get rid of it?
- What is one characteristic about the company's culture (or the internal work environment) that impairs our ability to quickly and effectively serve the customer?
- Where are internal issues with sales, service, fulfillment, or general operations caused by poor communi-

cations? What can be done to improve communications?
- What makes certain areas/departments in our organization operate in a silo? What could make them better team players?
- What is the one thing that leadership could do to make this organization more customer-centered?
- What is the one thing that I could do to make this organization more successful?

Throw out these questions to others, and use them yourself as a catalyst to get better and better.

Rate Yourself

Rate Your Level of Agreement:
3 = Strongly Agree, 2 = Agree, 1 = Do Not Agree

1. I am constantly looking for ways to improve how the work is done.
   Rating: _____

2. I have improved my own efficiency or the efficiency of my area with some changes implemented in the past three months.
   Rating: _____

3. I look for things to stop doing as much as I look for ways to do things better.
   Rating: _____

4. I have improved customer service or satisfaction in my area with some changes implemented in the past three months.
   Rating: _____

Total Chapter Score: _____

Record your Total Score in the "Calculate Your Greatness" table at the end of this Section.

Questions to Consider – Write Responses Below

Would you like things to stay just as they are now for the foreseeable future, or do you embrace change?

Do you look for ways to perform better?

Do you change with enough frequency that you can readily identify ways you are different or how you operate differently than you did six months ago?

Focus like a laser.

People Great at Customer Service...
Are Focused on the Other Person

When you're interacting with someone, where do you direct your attention? Individuals who are great at customer service never appear preoccupied in front of the customer. They are focused and engaged on the individual with whom they're interacting, as if that person is the most important person in the world to them at that moment in time.

Illustrating the point...
It's a scene that happens all the time. Several employees are working at their desks or behind a counter, absorbed with their computers. Customers are in line, being served one at a time, each by a different one of the employees. Finally, one customer is left, but nobody serves him. He stands and waits. And waits, and waits. After a round of throat-clearing, he is recognized. One employee responds, "Oh, I'm sorry. I assumed you were with someone else."

Let's cut to a different scene. The employee is working at his desk and gets a call from a customer about a project delay. The employee was looking at his computer prior to the call and continues to do so while the customer talks. At one point, the customer asks, "Are you listening to me?" To which the employee responds, "Oh...oh, yes, I'm sorry. What were you saying?"

The final scene features a representative at the video store. A customer walks in to see the employee doing his best Michael

Jackson moon walk, listening to his MP3 player with his head down as he restocks the shelves. "Excuse me," the customer says – and repeats. Finally she taps him on the shoulder, and he jumps two feet to his left. His response? "Sorry...what?"

In the first scene, the employee's focus is on the computer; in the second scene, it's on the computer; in the third scene, it's on that song blaring in his ear.

In all cases, the customer is frustrated, feeling ignored, not important.

Computers and other electronic devices may help you do your job or improve the work environment, but they are never more important than that customer who's in front of you or on the phone. The voice of the customer should be your trigger to turn away from those mesmerizing electronic devices, lest the customer assumes you to be rude, self-absorbed, indifferent, or inattentive.

Let the customer's voice be your trigger to turn away from the technology and focus on what's most important.

Rate Yourself

Rate Your Level of Agreement:
3 = Strongly Agree, 2 = Agree, 1 = Do Not Agree

1. When approached by a co-worker or customer, I focus my attention squarely on them (stopping other tasks if at all possible).
   Rating: _____

2. When I receive a phone call, I focus my attention squarely on the caller (stopping other tasks if at all possible).
   Rating: _____

3. I maintain effective eye contact with those with whom I am speaking.
   Rating: _____

4. I convey that I'm focused on the person through good body language and a tone of voice that shows I am engaged in the conversation.
   Rating: _____

Total Chapter Score: _____

Record your Total Score in the "Calculate Your Greatness" table at the end of this Section.

Questions to Consider – Write Responses Below

Are you fully engaged in conversations with others?

Can you forget about other things during that "Moment of Truth" so the customer feels like they're the most important person in the world to you right then?

How can you become more focused on the other person when engaged with others?

Do you realize they're all individuals?

People Great at Customer Service…
Empathize with the Customer

Empathy conveys understanding in a cognitive, intellectual way. Unlike sympathy, which implies that you understand exactly what another person's situation is and what they're going through at that moment in time, empathy conveys an understanding of *how* a person could feel that way, instead of exactly *what* they feel at that point in time.

Many customers react negatively to statements of sympathy such as *"I feel your pain"* or *"I've felt exactly what you're going through."* The customer reacts negatively because - in reality - you don't really understand <u>exactly</u> what they're going through and, therefore, the customer can be offended by what they perceive as your insincerity.

Instead of working toward sympathy, work toward understanding. Individuals who are great at customer service have a great capacity for empathy.

Illustrating the point…
Maybe it's the irate customer venting their disgust. Maybe it's the confused customer discussing their frustration. Maybe it's the upset customer detailing their ordeal. Whatever the situation, a little empathy can go a long way.

When presented with these emotional customers, if you don't react or respond, customers may think you're like a brick wall – an obstinate obstacle with no concern for their needs. If you argue their points, they stay emotional and think you are (to say it nicely) *rude*.

When presented with someone who's irate or upset or has a complaint, take the route of empathy. Essentially make a sincere statement: "I can understand your frustration" or "I can see how upsetting this must be." In doing that, you show that you're trying to be understanding of their emotions. They realize that you're not that brick wall; you're not that rude employee.

Instead, you're someone who listens, someone who understands. Keep in mind we're recommending empathy, not sympathy. Most people don't like statements of sympathy in situations like this because you don't know exactly what they're going through.

Think of the man who's in the delivery room with his wife; she just gave birth, and he turns to his wife and says "honey, I know exactly what you just went through."

Yikes!

That's sympathy. Don't do it. It's too big a risk. That might make them even more mad, even more upset.

Instead, when presented with the emotional customer, use a little empathy to help lower the emotions.

Rate Yourself

Rate Your Level of Agreement:
3 = Strongly Agree, 2 = Agree, 1 = Do Not Agree

1. I try to understand why the other person is saying what they are saying.
   Rating: _____

2. I convey to upset or irate people that their emotions are understandable.
   Rating: _____

3. I use effective body language characteristics such as the nodding of the head to convey understanding.
   Rating: _____

4. I use a tone of voice that conveys interest and caring.
   Rating: _____

Total Chapter Score: _____

Record your Total Score in the "Calculate Your Greatness" table at the end of this Section.

Questions to Consider – Write Responses Below

Do you try to understand others' perspectives?

Do you know the difference between understanding the other person without necessarily having to agree with the other person?

How can you become more empathetic?

Do you know everything already?

People Great at Customer Service...
Have a Learning Orientation

Individuals who are great at customer service are constantly learning – about themselves, their organization, their customers, about customer service in general.

Realize that there's much you don't know. Work to learn more from situations, co-workers, customers, leaders, and others' experiences. If you have the misconception that you know everything, consider that that ultimate knowledge is something you have for only for a brief period of time. Tomorrow the customers will change, or their needs will change, or the organization's priorities can change. Governmental pressures can change, processes can change, work volumes can change, personalities can change, or co-workers can change.

Even if you know everything about a situation at this very instant, the facts and circumstances *will change* over time. Knowledge needs to change to continue to be effective, and you will need to continue to learn in order to continually adapt to all the moving pieces that surround your working world.

Illustrating the point...
At one point in my work life, I was an internal consultant. An internal consultant is basically somebody with onsite responsibilities for project work five days a week all year long, as essentially an adopted employee of the organization.

The position to whom I reported in the organization was the Chief Operating Officer; a new person had just moved into that position. I met with this new COO, and we talked about what his goals were and how he wanted to utilize internal consulting support. During the conversation, I told him that if I did my job right, I would put myself out of a job. In other words, if we improved everything that needed to be improved upon, there'd be nothing left that warranted my expertise.

The COO appreciated the sentiment, but he responded that even if we did get the organization running as effectively as possible, they would always need to improve. Because even if everything worked perfectly for a given period of time, the next day things would be different. Maybe competitive pressures would change, maybe the technology or the funding sources would change. It could be that customers and their needs changed, or it could be that employees are hired or lost.

His point was that no organization can perform successfully at one point in time, then simply expect that it will continue to achieve success without growing and changing.

Organizations need to learn. Employees need to learn. What we know at any given moment is typically effective for that day and that time. However, if you want to be successful tomorrow in meeting the customer's expectations, if you want to deal successfully with new competitive pressures, if you want to relate to an ever-changing culture both inside and outside of the organization, *change is necessary.* You must constantly learn, constantly improve, constantly change your methods for the better.

Try to learn something new and apply it to your customer service approach every single day.

Rate Yourself

Rate Your Level of Agreement:
3 = Strongly Agree, 2 = Agree, 1 = Do Not Agree

1. I have learned something from a co-worker that I have applied within the last month.
   Rating: _____

2. I read something which has enabled me to operate, think, or act differently within the last month.
   Rating: _____

3. I have asked for feedback from a co-worker or a customer within the last week and applied that information.
   Rating: _____

4. I've noticed something in myself within the past month which I identified needs improvement.
   Rating: _____

Total Chapter Score: _____

Record your Total Score in the "Calculate Your Greatness" table at the end of this Section.

Questions to Consider – Write Responses Below

Do you love to learn?

Do you fear feedback or welcome it?

Can you look at yourself and identify things that you don't know?

How can you look for and act on opportunities to learn more?

Meet the co-workers.

People Great at Customer Service…
View Co-workers as Customers

Let us have a common definition of "customer." A customer is not simply some consumer who is paying you for a product or service. The customer is somebody to whom you provide something which enables them to move toward a goal. What you sell is not just a hamburger or an auto part or medication or a movie ticket; it is also the information, the education or the knowledge that moves another human being toward a goal.

Think of those people within your organization to whom you provide information, education or knowledge. If you do not provide these services in a timely manner, with a great attitude and in a simple fashion, that failure could result in your co-workers becoming that much less effective in doing what they do. Co-workers who rely on you are also your customers.

People who are great at customer service are great to ALL their customers, internal and external.

Illustrating the point...
Sometimes it's hard to think of co-workers as customers. But if you want to be customer service oriented, then know who your customers are, even if they are within your department.

Consider these questions:

- To whom in your department or organization do you give information?
- Who in your department or organization is impacted by your decisions?

- Who in your department or organization is impacted when you're slow to respond to a request?
- Who in your department or organization is impacted when your plans change, when there are errors in your work, or when you don't return phone calls?

Those people are your customers. They rely on you.

To deliver great customer service as an organization, we must first see how we impact each other as customers.

Rate Yourself

Rate Your Level of Agreement:
3 = Strongly Agree, 2 = Agree, 1 = Do Not Agree

1. I know specific co-workers who rely on me to provide them with information, products, materials, or services that they use to get their job done.
   Rating: _____

2. I know specific co-workers who I rely on to provide me with information, products, materials, or services that I use to get my job done.
   Rating: _____

3. I understand if my work gets delayed how it impacts those co-workers who rely on me.
   Rating: _____

4. I understand how – if the quality of my work is not high – it impacts others.
   Rating: _____

Total Chapter Score: _____

Record your Total Score in the "Calculate Your Greatness" table at the end of this Section.

Questions to Consider – Write Responses Below

Are you as responsive to co-workers as you are to external customers?

Do you realize the impact you have on your co-workers' ability to do their jobs?

Do you try to help your co-workers succeed by delivering what they request of you?

Do you fear confrontation?

People Great at Customer Service…
Are Willing to Share Bad News

Individuals who are great at customer service realize that one of the most important times to be proactive is when there is bad news to share. Let us take a totally selfish view of this. Let's say that you find out some bad news impacting a co-worker or customer. Maybe their request is backordered, or their project is behind schedule.

If they find out about this before you tell them, then that makes them the ones who have to initiate the conversation with you. There will most likely be some negative emotion when customers become aware of something bad about which you were aware, but had failed to tell them. Now you not only have to deal with the issue, but you're engaged in a conversation with somebody who's upset, angry, even irate. Since they were forced to initiate the conversation, you are reacting to them and their emotion while ceding control of the conversation.

Let me emphasize the point: An *angry customer* is in control of your conversation.

When you become aware of bad news, you must be proactive in sharing it with the customer who is affected. Take the lead, so that you have control over how bad news is presented and in what environment it is presented. Doing so will enable you to think through possible reactions, and to be able to guide the conversation from the start toward a less emotional and more logical ending.

When it comes to discussing Bad News, be the first to bring it up with the customer or co-worker.

Illustrating the point...

A friend of mine told me this story, and he got it from a friend, so I'm not sure of its true origins. To the original storyteller, I say thank you, whoever you are...

A successful CEO was getting near retirement age and knew it was time to begin the selection process for a successor to take over the business. He decided to use a unique selection process, however. He called all the young executives in his company together. He told them that he was nearing the end of his career and would soon step down. The young executives were surprised and disappointed. The CEO then said, "It is time for me to begin determining my successor. I have decided to choose one of you."

The other executives were shocked. The CEO continued, "I am going to give each one of you a seed today – one very special seed. I want you to plant the seed, water it, and come back here one year from today with what you have grown from the seed I have given you. I will then judge the plants that you bring, and the one I choose will be the next CEO."

One of the young executives named Chuck took his seed, went home, and told his wife. She helped him get a pot, add some good dirt, some plant food, and he planted the seed. Every day, he watered it and watched to see if it had grown.

It hadn't.

After about three weeks, some of the other executives began to talk about their seeds and the plants that were beginning to grow. Chuck's never grew. Month after month, after all the watering, tending to the soil, and proper exposure to light, nothing happened. The other young executives continued to talk of their beautiful, thriving plants.

Chuck had a pot full of dirt.

Once the year had finally passed, the CEO told the young executives to bring in the results of their efforts for review. Chuck almost didn't want to go in to work, but his wife encouraged him to bring in the pot, explain the effort, and be honest about his lack of results.

When all the executives arrived in the Boardroom, each executive had a beautiful plant, and all were different sizes and beautiful colors.

Chuck had his pot full of dirt.

When the CEO arrived, he surveyed the room and greeted his young executives. "My, what great plants you have grown," said the CEO. He then looked quizzically at Chuck. "Everybody sit down, please – except Chuck," said the CEO. "What happened, Chuck?" asked the CEO.

Chuck told his story.

The CEO then turned to the others and said "Behold your next Chief Executive! His name is Chuck!"

What?

Then the CEO said, "One year ago today, I gave everyone in this room a seed. I told you to take the seed, plant it, water it, and bring it back to me today. But I gave you all boiled seeds; they were dead – it was not possible for them to grow. All of you, except Chuck, have brought me plants. Chuck was the only one with the courage and honesty to bring me a pot with my seed in it."

How does this relate to the world of customer service? You can earn a great deal of respect for yourself, from family, and from those that matter most if you have the courage to be honest.

Have the courage to tell the bad news.

Rate Yourself

Rate Your Level of Agreement:
3 = Strongly Agree, 2 = Agree, 1 = Do Not Agree

1. I initiate conversations with others about bad news that I or my area may have caused.
   Rating: _____

2. I am open to receiving criticism when there is an issue with my work or the work of my department or company.
   Rating: _____

3. I understand the position that the other person is in when there is a concern with my work or the work of my department or company.
   Rating: _____

4. I understand the need to discuss the issue instead of delaying the discussion until I can devise the perfect solution.
   Rating: _____

Total Chapter Score: _____

Record your Total Score in the "Calculate Your Greatness" table at the end of this Section.

Questions to Consider – Write Responses Below

Do you understand how initiating "Bad News" discussions with customers or others who rely on you can actually benefit you?

Do you understand how initiating "Bad News" discussions with customers or others who rely on you can benefit the other person?

How can you get better at initiating these conversations?

Calculate Your Greatness – Is Your Attitude Great?

Enter your total score from the chapter noted below in the spaces provided to the right.

How full is the cup?　　　　　　　　Total Chapter Score: _____

What's the balance in your knowledge bank?　　　　　　Total Chapter Score: _____

Patience...patience...　　　　　　Total Chapter Score: _____

Set aside the status quo.　　　　　Total Chapter Score: _____

Focus like a laser.　　　　　　　　Total Chapter Score: _____

Do you realize they're an individual?　　　　　　　　　Total Chapter Score: _____

Do you know everything already?　Total Chapter Score: _____

Meet the co-workers.　　　　　　　Total Chapter Score: _____

Do you fear confrontation?　　　　Total Chapter Score: _____

Add Total Chapter Scores to Get Your Total Section Score: _____

Interpreting Your Scores...

100-108 - You have a GREAT customer service attitude!

91-99 - You have many of the key qualities required to be great. You definitely have a good attitude.

Under 91 - There's work to be done.

Needing to improve? Look back to the chapters where you scored lowest and focus on the tips and questions. You can also get a more personal detailed assessment with recommendations at www.amigreatat.com.

Are You Great When You're In Front of the Customer?

Here it is. Face-to-face or on the phone. Don't let them see you sweat. They ask the question; you must respond. They complain; you must react. It's either a dialogue or it's an issue on the precipice of becoming an argument. Maybe that first impression is your only chance to impress.

It's a *Moment of Truth*.

How do you handle it? The customer immediately knows how you handled it. They immediately have an impression of whether you're great…or not.

Think before you speak?

People Great at Customer Service...
Choose Their Words Effectively

What you say and how you project yourself impact how others view you. Maybe the words themselves are not the primary determinant of the opinion that others have of you personally, but the words matter.

The words state whether you're a thoughtful individual, whether you're empathetic toward the other person, whether you have a working knowledge of your organization, and whether or not you have a working knowledge of the customer situation as well.

Therefore, use the words you choose in such a way that you're building trust, confidence, and credibility in the mind of the other person.

What you say matters, and individuals great at customer service are thoughtful in what they say.

Illustrating the point...
Steve brought his golf shoes into the pro shop to get new spikes. The current spikes were so old that he couldn't unscrew them. When Steve showed the shoes to the sales person and asked if he could replace the spikes, that employee could have responded "I'm not sure" or "I don't think so" or "Maybe" or "Ugh." But, instead, he responded "I hope so. Let me try."

All five of those potential statements showed uncertainty, but the last one used by the employee included wording that conveyed a positive nature, hope, and a willingness to take the next step and try.

A customer comes into your store with an item to return that was bought 32 days ago (you have a 30-day return policy). Do you respond with "I'm not sure we can take that" or "Wow, that's really late" or "I hope we can take it back. Let me see what I can do for you?"

The client calls in and asks if you can expedite the deliverable to them. Do you respond "I don't know" or "That's awfully tight" or "But it's not due for another week" or "Let me check and see what we can do for you."

The golf spike example is one that requires effort on the part of the employee to accomplish a task. The item return example is one that deals with addressing a potential conflict with policy. The client deliverable example is one that deals with a change in internal timeframes. Although they all deal with different topics, each requires that an employee respond with uncertainty because he or she does not know the answer yet. Maybe the employee can do what the customer wants, or maybe not.

This is not to say that you should promise that you CAN do something when you cannot. If you did so, you would be promoting unrealistic expectations.

But what we ARE saying is that you can respond with uncertainty and still give hope. You can respond with uncertainty and show that you'll make the effort. You can respond with uncertainty and create a positive climate for the conversation.

Deal with uncertainty in your response with hope and a next step. Give it a try.

Rate Yourself

Rate Your Level of Agreement:
3 = Strongly Agree, 2 = Agree, 1 = Do Not Agree

1. I speak with honesty and sincerity.
   Rating: _____

2. I use my words to convey an appropriate sense of hope, even with uncertainty.
   Rating: _____

3. I speak with the intent to say what I am saying, choosing my words prior to speaking them.
   Rating: _____

4. I try to understand the other person's mindset and situation, tailoring my words to be most useful and effective.
   Rating: _____

Total Chapter Score: _____

Record your Total Score in the "Calculate Your Greatness" table at the end of this Section.

Am I Great at Customer Service?

Questions to Consider – Write Responses Below

Is there any filter between what you think and what you say?

Do you think about the recipient of the information when deciding how to say what you need to say?

How can you become better at tailoring your message?

Your actions speak so loudly that...

People Great at Customer Service...
Are Effective Non-Verbal Communicators

People who are great at customer service understand that a key to effective communication is the ability to convey respect for another person with body language and tone of voice. Studies have shown that, until they really get familiar with each other, over 90% of people will primarily judge another person based on how that person comes across with body language and tone of voice.

With these communication attributes, you can come off as interested or disinterested, as upset or understanding, as pre-occupied or present, as patient or impatient, as informal or unprofessional.

People who are great at customer service have a great awareness of how they come across with body language and tone of voice, and they use that awareness to make a positive impact.

Illustrating the point...
When daylight savings time occurs, it's a semi-annual reminder to change the batteries in your smoke detectors. As I was going through that process last year, I realized that there was a room in the house where I assumed we had a smoke detector but didn't. I don't think it just got up and walked off to find greener pastures, so it's obviously not one of my brighter intellectual moments. But, regardless, I needed one for that room.

So I went to the local big box home improvement store where they claim to be all about customer service. After not finding the smoke detector I wanted, I walked up to a gentleman who worked there. As I got near him, it was as if he could sense that I was approaching to ask a question, and he began to walk away! Eventually he stopped, looked at me with a blank stare and didn't say a word. I said, "Excuse me, Sir, but do you know where the smoke detectors are?"

He then turned and walked away from me, and I followed. He walked out of that aisle, around a corner, down another aisle, moved a ladder-on-wheels, and stood there, in front of the smoke detectors. He had a blank look and didn't say a word. I smiled and said, "Thanks!" He turned and walked away.

It was odd, but I've had a few of those non-verbal experiences before. Maybe he couldn't talk, or maybe he wasn't confident, or maybe he was painfully shy. What was good about the situation was that I was directed to the location I needed. But there were a lot of negative layers to that experience. One such negativity was that I now stood in front of literally a dozen different types of smoke detectors with nobody to help me.

I've always been a shy person. Even though I'm not nearly as shy as I used to be, in dealing with others shy people can often come off as being rude, uncaring or disinterested. Yet shy people can be some of the most caring people around; they may just not be comfortable or confident enough to initiate conversations, engage customers, and ask questions.

Fair or not, customers form perceptions based on their experiences. Those perceptions influence opinions which in turn influence repeat business and word-of-mouth.

Many of the perceptions are based on non-verbal communication. That is all I got from this employee, and those non-verbal communications were not good. He walked away initially (conveying "I don't want to talk with you, Mr. Customer"); he didn't smile ("I'm not happy to help"); he had a blank look ("I'm doing my task; that's all I care about"); he left as soon as I said thanks ("I'm impatient and have better things to do than to ensure you get exactly what you need").

Make sure that your body language creates a positive customer perception.

Rate Yourself

Rate Your Level of Agreement:
3 = Strongly Agree, 2 = Agree, 1 = Do Not Agree

1. I am very aware of how I come across with my body language when I am communicating with someone face-to-face.
   Rating: _____

2. I utilize my body language and expressions to convey interest and respect.
   Rating: _____

3. I am very aware of how I come across with my tone of voice when I am communicating with someone.
   Rating: _____

4. I utilize my voice to convey interest and respect.
   Rating: _____

Total Chapter Score: _____

Record your Total Score in the "Calculate Your Greatness" table at the end of this Section.

Questions to Consider – Write Responses Below

Do you know how you come across to others with your body language and expressions?

Do you know how you come across to others with your tone of voice?

Do you use body language and tone of voice to convey the message you want to convey in an appropriate manner?

Do you think about how you use these non-verbal characteristics during interactions with others?

What about your body language or tone of voice do you need to improve?

Here comes a call!

People Great at Customer Service…
Use Effective Call Handling Techniques

Handling customer calls is an art. Like many pieces of art during the wars that have raged over the years on this globe, the art of handling customer calls has become damaged, if not outright lost. It's not that there are people who stole or destroyed effective call handling skills the way the art was stolen and destroyed, but too many organizations have lacked focus on the impact of poor call handling on customer satisfaction, and on the company's long-term success.

There is nothing more aggravating to a customer than being transferred three times and having to repeat himself to three different employees. And there is no worse position for an employee to be in than having to deal with a customer who's already upset and has been made more upset because of the process of getting to that employee.

People who are great at customer service understand the impact that call handling can have on the customer's mindset.

Illustrating the point...
In football, it's said that when a quarterback hands off the football to the running back, it's the quarterback's responsibility to make sure that the ball is in the running back's stomach, between his arms. The effective handoff is the quarterback's responsibility – the running back is focused on where there's an opening to run or where the defensive players are during the play. If there's a bad handoff, it's the quarterback's fault.

The same holds true when there's a handoff of a caller from one employee to another. The responsibility for that caller's conversation with the co-worker to begin well is that of the person making the transfer to the co-worker. If Mary is transferring to Tim, it's Mary's responsibility to put Tim in a position to be successful.

Here are some keys to the effective call transfer. Mary should:

- Avoid the use of the word *transfer* with the customer. This word has a very negative connotation in society today. Many people translate "I'm transferring you to..." as "You're not worth my time. I'm going to pass you off to someone else." Instead, you should say: "I am going to connect you with..."

- Explain why she's connecting the caller with someone else. The caller needs to understand the rationale behind the new connection and accept it. The caller must realize that it's not because Mary doesn't care, but rather that Mary wants to put the caller in touch with the person who can best help. This builds Tim's credibility in the mind of the customer.

- Give the caller Tim's name and direct number. The last thing Mary wants is for the caller to call her back just to get put back on hold and transferred again. Giving Tim's name also personalizes the call for the next discussion.

- If the phone system makes it possible, stay on the line and introduce Tim to the caller. Attempt to let Tim know in advance that a call is coming, from whom, and why. This prepares Tim for the discussion he's about to

have, and that way the customer doesn't have to repeat everything.
- If necessary based on the call content, ask the caller if there's anything else they need help with prior to the new connection. This conveys patience and ensures that all of the customer's needs are met.

Don't fumble the ball on a transfer/connection. Use these guidelines to make the effective handoff.

Rate Yourself

Rate Your Level of Agreement:
3 = Strongly Agree, 2 = Agree, 1 = Do Not Agree

1. I avoid using the word "transfer" when I have to connect the caller with someone else.
   Rating: _____

2. I explain why I am having to connect them with a co-worker.
   Rating: _____

3. I give the caller the option to leave a message with me or be connected with the co-worker's voice mail if they're not available.
   Rating: _____

4. I try to stay on the line and introduce the caller or – at a minimum – tell the co-worker whom I'm sending to them.
   Rating: _____

Total Chapter Score: _____

Record your Total Score in the "Calculate Your Greatness" table at the end of this Section.

Questions to Consider – Write Responses Below

Are you more concerned with moving a call along or with effectively getting the caller in touch with the right person the first time?

Do you make a conscious effort to put your co-worker in a positive position if you send a call to them?

How can you improve your call handling?

Listen up!

People Great at Customer Service…
Converse Well

During the course of a conversation, many customers judge your service orientation based on two key factors. Primary, of course, is the First Impression. Do you come across as focused on and interested in the other individual, or do you come across as rude, self-focused, indifferent, or preoccupied?

The second key aspect of a conversation that customers use to judge you is your Closing. Is your closing one where you communicate appreciation for the customer, or is the closing more along the lines of "no problem," which essentially says "You're not a problem to me"? Is there a "thank you" initiated by the employee or is there dead silence, where the customer feels like they have to initiate the thanks?

Individuals who are great at customer service make sure that when they're communicating with others, they're communicating by making a great impression at the start, and by showing appreciation at the close.

Our company does a tremendous amount of mystery shopping. Whether mystery shops are face-to-face discussions or telephone conversations, the best mystery shops invariably involve employees who are inquisitive about the customer. During your conversations with your customers, ask enough questions to understand the customer's true situation so that you can very specifically and directly answer correctly the first time. This is another key to making the customer think "Wow! That employee was great!"

Am I Great at Customer Service?

Illustrating the point...

It was the late 1980's, and there was a boxing match between two fighters – Sugar Ray Leonard and Marvelous Marvin Hagler. A typical round went like this:

The bell rang. Sugar Ray came out on fire. He was dancin'. He was jabbin'. He was wowing the crowd with his boxing prowess for the first 15-30 seconds of each round. Then – for the next 2 minutes or 2 minutes and 15 seconds of the round – the fight would slow down. Hagler would start to take control. The fight would become more of a plodding fight with less excitement and movement.

Then – with about 15-30 seconds left in the round – Sugar Ray would take over again. He would just light up! The footwork was there; the crowd went wild, and then the bell would ring.

Ding! Ding!

If you looked at the punch statistics at the end of the fight, Hagler threw far more punches. Hagler connected on far more punches. But if you looked at the judges' scorecards, Sugar Ray Leonard won.

Leonard won because the judges were scoring the rounds based more upon how the rounds started and how they ended than upon their plodding middles, and Sugar Ray won the starts and the ends of the rounds.

So what does this have to do with customer service?

When customers evaluate how you handled their request, when they're asked how service-oriented you were, much of what they'll base their response on is the way you started and ended the conversation. That first impression and that close of the conversation make a huge difference in the customer's overall perception of how you handled his or her request.

If you want to score high in the customer's eyes, make sure you open strong and close strong.

Rate Yourself

Rate Your Level of Agreement:
3 = Strongly Agree, 2 = Agree, 1 = Do Not Agree

1. I stop what I'm doing when engaged by a customer, and pleasantly greet them.
   Rating: _____

2. I ask questions and confirm my understanding of their needs prior to addressing them.
   Rating: _____

3. I ensure they got their needs met and confirm their satisfaction before closing conversations.
   Rating: _____

4. I convey appreciation for their business and/or their comments at the end of conversations.
   Rating: _____

Total Chapter Score: _____

Record your Total Score in the "Calculate Your Greatness" table at the end of this Section.

Questions to Consider – Write Responses Below

Do you try to make a great impression at the start of conversations?

Do you intently listen to the other person?

Do you consistently close conversations positively and/or with a statement of appreciation?

They're angry. What are you going to do?

People Great at Customer Service...
Defuse the Upset/Irate Customer

When employees deal with somebody who has a complaint, is upset or even irate, employees who are great in these situations are typically individuals who can accomplish two things. They are able to reduce the emotional level of the customer while gaining control of the conversation.

People who are great at customer service are able to reduce the emotional level of the irate customer. It is so much easier to have a conversation with somebody who is calm than to deal with somebody who is emotional.

Customer service professionals who are great in these situations also gain control of the conversation in an appropriate manner. They keep in mind that when the complaint starts, it is usually initiated by the customer venting or complaining; they are sharing emotion, and the employee must react to that emotion.

The irate customer is in control. In these situations, however, *you* want to be the one in control. Employees who are great with disgruntled customers are great at gaining control of the conversation.

Illustrating the point...
As part of an engagement with a client seven or eight years ago, we conducted customer service training. The training involved a technique that helps to defuse the upset customer. We taught

the technique to the participants, and then we broke them up into small groups to do some role-playing. Once we launched these employee breakout sessions, we immediately took notice of a group in the left corner of the room. The complaining customer was a big guy, and he was being obnoxious and loud. He was really getting into the role of being the angry customer!

The other role plays in the room began to stop as everyone started watching the group in the corner.

As the trainers in this session, we watched that group in the corner and thought, *How in the world is the employee going to handle this guy?*

Here is what the employee was doing:

He just made eye contact with the customer, and occasionally he would nod. The employee didn't say a word; he just stayed *focused on* and *listened to* the customer. He was letting the customer go, letting him vent, letting him blow off a little steam.

Then the employee finally spoke. He asked a simple question, "Now did that happen on Tuesday or on Thursday?"

You could see the "customer" stop dead in his tracks. He looked around and thought for a couple seconds, and then he said "Well, I...I think it happened on Tuesday."

He then tried to go back into his complaint, but he had lost a lot of steam. Because in the middle of all this emotion and all this upset, he was forced to answer a logical question. And it is very difficult to maintain the emotion and upset and to think and respond logically and factually at the same time.

So the next time you're in front of somebody who's upset and complaining about something, get them to think logically, factually, objectively. Ask those "A versus B" questions, or ask for a fact or a figure (like the account number, the address, the name, the dollar amount).

Simply put, it is very difficult to maintain a high emotional level while having to think and respond logically and factually at the same time.

Rate Yourself

Rate Your Level of Agreement:
3 = Strongly Agree, 2 = Agree, 1 = Do Not Agree

1. I listen well upfront in these situations, letting the customer vent, and only asking questions when I speak.
   Rating: _____

2. I ask objective questions to gain facts and to get the customer to think.
   Rating: _____

3. I convey empathy and convey that I'm sorry about their situation.
   Rating: _____

4. I identify and deliver on remedies to issues and complaints.
   Rating: _____

Total Chapter Score: _____

Record your Total Score in the "Calculate Your Greatness" table at the end of this Section.

Questions to Consider – Write Responses Below

Do you allow the person ample time to vent?

Do you avoid the urge to argue with the upset or angry customer?

Do you ask close-ended questions in these situations?

Do you avoid discussing blame and – instead – focus on the issue and possible solutions?

How could you get better at dealing with these tough conversations?

I want to be King of the World!

People Great at Customer Service...
Effectively Set and Manage Expectations

Customer service studies have shown that almost half of customer dissatisfaction results from a customer expecting one thing but getting something else. Maybe the sales staff or marketing materials overpromised. Maybe the company, its people, its processes, or its products didn't do even the minimum of what the customer expected.

Any way you slice it, managing customer expectations or setting appropriate expectations enables employees to reduce the number of complaints and conflicts they receive.

Successfully accomplishing one of two actions will help you to manage those expectations properly. First, you want to appropriately set expectations with the customer about how long something will take, what the process will be like, what you'll be doing, and what they need to do.

Second, it's important to determine what the customer expects. If those expectations are not realistic, you need to manage that customer's expectations closer to reality.

Individuals who are great at customer service do an effective job of setting and managing customer expectations.

Illustrating the point...
We bought a used car on a Friday. We still owned our previous car (hadn't sold it yet), but decided to take a trip to Atlanta

from Charlotte with our "new used" car, mainly because our "old used" car was a lemon.

About a hundred miles into the trip, the "check engine" light went on. Yes, the new used car was signaling me that it would be no different from my old used car. Another car, another source of stress.

Then the car began to buck, and since the bull-riding experience is never one I've craved, I found this a rather unpleasant turn of events.

The first opportunity to get the car looked at was at 7:00 a.m. on Monday. Arriving at 6:45 a.m. to be first in line, I was happy to see the service area open right on time. The Assistant Service Manager said that by 8:30 a.m. my issue would be diagnosed. At 9:15 a.m., expecting the worst after receiving no communication since I first sat down in the waiting room, I went to the Assistant Service Manager for an update. Luckily, my car was only going to require a minor repair, which was mostly covered by warranty.

So what was the issue? *Expectation management.* If you have one hundred customers but don't set a consistent expectation for the service level, those one hundred customers will have one hundred different expectations. You won't meet many of the expectations, but you will have a lot of unnecessarily irate customers.

When you set service expectations, manage them well. In my case, an update had been promised by 8:30. I expected that update to come at that time, but it didn't come until I sought it out at 9:15. During that conversation, the employee noted that the car would be ready at 10:15. At 11:00, having heard not a word in almost two hours, I went to the Assistant Service Manager *again* for an update! Regardless of how well they fixed the car, I was disappointed overall with the experience because they gave me one expectation but delivered a different reality.

The difference between expectations and reality can be defined as a problem. In customer service terms, that problem results in bad word of mouth, customer loss, and complaints.

Cut your risk of customer dissatisfaction by better setting and managing customer expectations.

Rate Yourself

Rate Your Level of Agreement:
3 = Strongly Agree, 2 = Agree, 1 = Do Not Agree

1. I convey to the customer what to expect if they haven't already shared their expectation with me.
   Rating: _____

2. I ask what they expect if we haven't discussed it.
   Rating: _____

3. I attempt to adjust their expectation prior to taking action if their expectation is unrealistic.
   Rating: _____

4. I confirm we're on the same page about next steps and timeframes before closing conversations.
   Rating: _____

Total Chapter Score: _____

Record your Total Score in the "Calculate Your Greatness" table at the end of this Section.

Questions to Consider – Write Responses Below

Do you look for ways to set appropriate expectations with the customer regarding what type of experience they will have?

At the end of conversations, do you confirm with the other person what the next steps are and when they are expected to happen?

How can you get better at ensuring customers and co-workers have realistic expectations?

Calculate Your Greatness – Are You Great When You're In Front of the Customer?

Enter your total score from the chapter noted below in the spaces provided to the right.

Think before you speak?   Total Chapter Score: _____

Your actions speak so loudly that… Total Chapter Score: _____

Here comes a call!   Total Chapter Score: _____

Listen up!   Total Chapter Score: _____

They're angry. What are you going to do? Total Chapter Score: _____

I want to be King of the World!   Total Chapter Score: _____

Add Total Chapter Scores to Get Your Total Section Score: _____

Interpreting Your Scores…

    67-72 - You are GREAT in front of a customer!

  61-66 - You have many of the key qualities required to be great in front of a customer.

    Under 61 - There's work to be done.

Needing to improve? Look back to the chapters where you scored lowest and focus on the tips and questions. You can also get a more personal detailed assessment with recommendations at www.amigreatat.com.

Are You Great When the Customer's <u>Not</u> in Front of You?

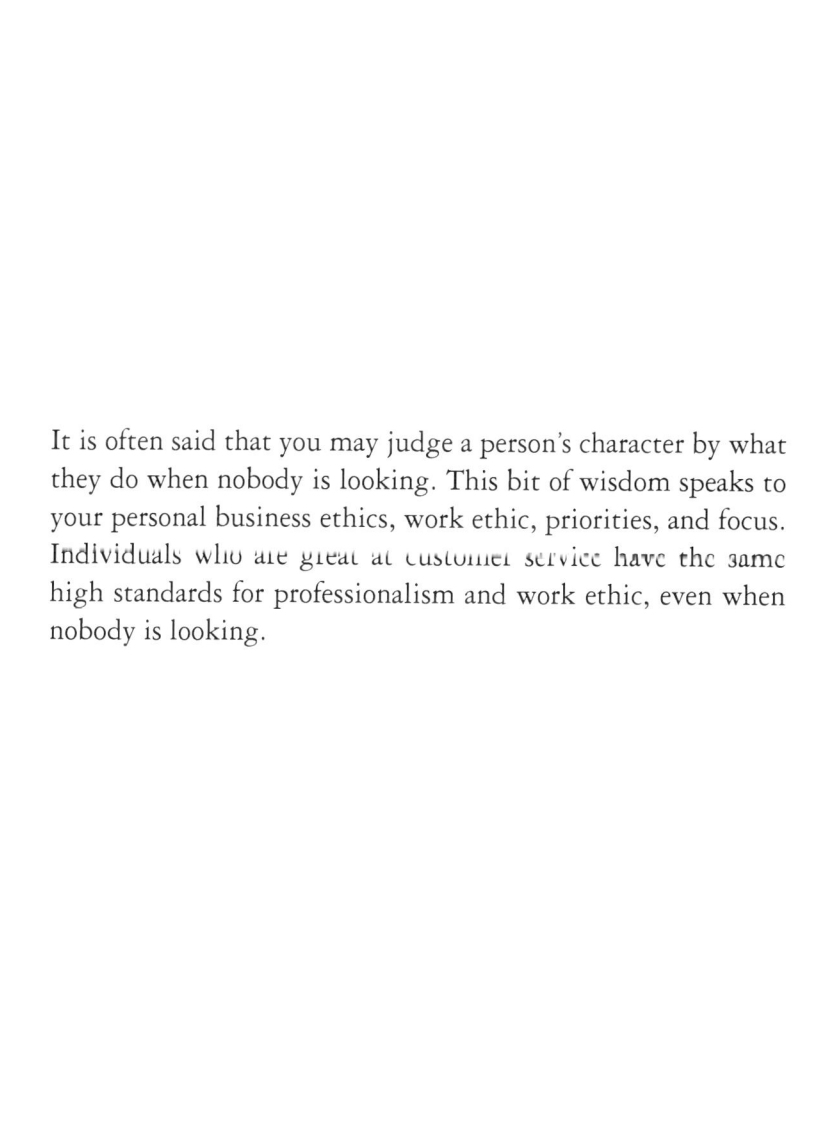

It is often said that you may judge a person's character by what they do when nobody is looking. This bit of wisdom speaks to your personal business ethics, work ethic, priorities, and focus. Individuals who are great at customer service have the same high standards for professionalism and work ethic, even when nobody is looking.

Find the common ground.

People Great at Customer Service...
Know How to Build Relationships

Are you a good teammate?

Individuals who are great at customer service realize the interconnectivity that different groups, different departments, and different individuals must have in order to meet a common goal. They realize how important it is to meet the needs of their co-workers so that they can address their customers' needs as well. They understand how important it is to provide the same high level of customer service to a co-worker that they provide to the end customer. They appreciate that the performance of the organization must be greater than the performance of the its individual parts.

People who are great at customer service are great teammates.

Illustrating the point...
Have you ever heard of the term *suboptimize*? If so, you probably understand that it is not necessarily a good thing. The concept of suboptimization can be illustrated in the following example.

Let's say that a business has five different departments, each of which is exceptionally effective on its own. However, organizationally, the company's performance could be poor.

The Purchasing and Materials Management areas' primary goal is to operate at the lowest possible cost per unit. The Operations area's goal is to do things as quickly as possible. Marketing's goal is to acquire customers in as large numbers as possible. Finally, the Customer Service area is trying to retain customers and grow with them.

Each one of these four areas can be exceptionally good at what they do, yet the organization could be performing exceptionally poorly.

For example, to get the lowest cost per unit, Purchasing may acquire items in bulk, which can allow the inventory levels to drop precipitously until they get the best deal. Therefore, the Operations area may not get the supplies they need as quickly as they are needed in order to perform their activities.

Materials Management may be trying to operate at a lower cost per unit by having minimal staffing, while at the same time Customer Service needs a quick delivery or a quick shipment to address customer needs or a repair issue. With a smaller workforce, there may not be the staff available to enable that issue to be resolved quickly.

It is also possible that the Operations area is trying to move at such a quick pace that they are making many errors. These mistakes can result in customers complaining about product or service-oriented issues – which increases the workload for the Customer Service area.

Maybe Marketing is trying to acquire as many new customers as possible, but the way that they do it is to offer perks, benefits, or pricing that cannot be sustained long-term; therefore, they may end up setting expectations that the rest of the organization cannot meet, which results in a high level of customer turnover.

In one last example, Customer Service may be so focused on retention of existing clients that they make urgent demands on the Operations area, demands which require Operations to stop their daily activities to meet that rushed need. This could slow down the Operations area's ability to efficiently perform their job since they're constantly getting interrupted.

For an organization to be successful, there need to be common goals and common motivating forces throughout that organization. To accomplish this, a willingness and desire must be fostered within the company to develop relationships with co-workers and other departments. Organizations that are effective at meeting the ultimate companywide goals of financial performance, quality, and customer satisfaction and loyalty, have that organization-wide mindset of *How can I help my co-workers to serve their customers? How can I get to know the priorities of other departments so that I can help make them successful? How can I communicate with other departments in such a way that they want to help me out?*

See how relating to other areas more effectively can help you to be more successful in your area in the long-run.

Rate Yourself

Rate Your Level of Agreement:
3 = Strongly Agree, 2 = Agree, 1 = Do Not Agree

1. I work with a team mindset with co-workers.
   Rating: _____

2. I treat co-workers with the same high level of respect and responsiveness that I treat my customers.
   Rating: _____

3. I look for ways to help my co-workers to be successful.
   Rating: _____

4. I view actions or information requested by co-workers with the same urgency that I would if it had come from an external customer.
   Rating: _____

Total Chapter Score: _____

Record your Total Score in the "Calculate Your Greatness" table at the end of this Section.

Questions to Consider – Write Responses Below

Are you truly a team player, carrying your load on your team or in your division/department?

Do co-workers feel like there are no silos dividing you from them?

Do you trust co-workers by sharing information and advice to help them succeed?

Do you pitch-in to help co-workers when needed?

To be or not to be...in touch.

People Great at Customer Service...
Are Responsive

Individuals who are great at customer service are responsive to their customer's needs. They respond to e-mails within six business hours and respond to voicemails if at all possible by the end of the day. They hear a need, and they address that need quickly. If there is an issue identified, they attempt to resolve that issue or complaint on the spot if at all possible.

If you are great at customer service, you are action-oriented.

Illustrating the point...
Jeremy was frustrated. He had sent an e-mail to Will, his account representative, to solve a billing issue and hadn't heard back in four days. This was the last straw, after a second billing issue in two months, yet another late delivery, and now even Jeremy's representative is ignoring him.

The next day, Jeremy called a competitor and placed a large order.

Later that day, Will called back.

- Will: Hi Jeremy. This is Will with Acme Paper Plus.
- Jeremy: Yes.
- Will: Great news! We not only got that invoice corrected, but I got you a 5% discount on your next purchase!
- Jeremy: Well that won't help.
- Will: What do you mean?

- Jeremy: I just made my next purchase...with your competitor.
- Will: Why? I've been working on your issue ever since I received your e-mail.
- Jeremy: How was I supposed to know that, Will? You never responded to my message.

Acme Paper Plus lost Jeremy as a customer. The last straw was not Will ignoring Jeremy's issue. Rather, the last straw was Will not acknowledging Jeremy's e-mail.

When you don't acknowledge e-mail and voice mail messages, customers may feel that they're not important, or that you dropped the ball, or that you might not have received the message, or that you're not working on it.

Realize the importance of acknowledgement to take control of the customer's expectations. Acknowledge the message, note the next steps, and provide a timeframe.

If you're working on the customer's behalf, make sure the customer realizes that.

Rate Yourself

Rate Your Level of Agreement:
3 = Strongly Agree, 2 = Agree, 1 = Do Not Agree

1. I quickly communicate to the sender of a message that I've received the request, even if I cannot address the request quickly.
   Rating: _____

2. When communicating with customers, I am clear about next steps and by when they'll occur.
   Rating: _____

3. I act on needs and issues within the customer's expectation.
   Rating: _____

4. If I'm out of the office, I clearly state on my voice and e-mail messages how the person can get their question answered if they cannot wait for my response.
   Rating: _____

Total Chapter Score: _____

Record your Total Score in the "Calculate Your Greatness" table at the end of this Section.

Questions to Consider – Write Responses Below

Would virtually anyone with whom you have contact consider you to be a responsive person?

Do you acknowledge messages that require follow-up, even if you cannot immediately resolve them?

How could you be more responsive to others?

Don't drop the ball.

People Great at Customer Service...
Follow-Up and Follow-Through

Individuals who are great at customer service do what they say they will do. That is the definition of follow-through. The conversation has ended, the transaction is over, and additional steps are discussed. Those great at customer service understand how to follow-through. They understand the importance of building trust by doing what they said they would do.

Follow-up is somewhat different. Follow-up deals with situations where a customer has a concern or a need. The employee hands off that customer and their need to a co-worker. Follow-up is when the first employee contacts the customer to ensure that the need was addressed or the issue was resolved to their satisfaction by the second employee.

Follow-up is an after-the-fact action that confirms that the intended action was taken or that the intended outcome was realized.

Illustrating the point...

Follow-Up
Jennifer had dealt with this situation many times. The client needed to talk to Accounting to get this issue addressed. So Jennifer, knowing this client in particular needed quick action, transferred the call to Scott in the Accounting department. Jennifer felt good that she was able to get the client in contact with Accounting as soon as possible. This was an important client,

and Jennifer was responsible for retaining the client. Jennifer felt like she had accomplished her task.

Two weeks later, Jennifer received an e-mail from the client. It stated that the client had canceled his agreement with the company, and the client noted how the billing issue had never been resolved with Accounting, and that was the main reason why he had left. The client had been thoroughly frustrated with the billing issues that had never been resolved.

Jennifer was furious. Jennifer blamed Accounting, but Jennifer was only *partially* correct. Jennifer did what she needed to do by transferring the call to Scott.

But keep in mind that the ultimate responsibility for retaining the client fell to Jennifer, and even though she trusted her co-worker to do his job, a simple follow-up with Scott or with the client soon after the call would have made it readily apparent whether or not that transfer had gotten the desired results. Jennifer didn't follow up, Scott didn't follow through, and the client canceled.

We need to trust our co-workers, but we also need to follow up to ensure satisfaction.

Follow-Through

Desiree was great in sales. It was amazing how she could take a client that was on the edge of buying or walking away, and convince that client to sign on the dotted line less than an hour later. It was a gift, although she had gone through much training, you could tell she had "It" from the start.

There was an issue, however. Even though Desiree could close a very high percentage of her opportunities, she always had the highest attrition rate of all the sales personnel. She had far more cancellations in the first year of the contract than any of the other sales representatives.

One of the biggest issues that most customers brought up is that she made a lot of promises to close the deals. And these were not unusual promises. Rather, they were the same promises that others in the organization made as well.

They were promises of monthly visits. They were promises of quarterly reports on the return on investment to the client. They were promises of occasional upgrades in services when available. And although the core company products and services were delivered to the client, Desiree – after that initial sales transaction – was terrible at follow-through. She did not effectively follow-through on what she promised to do, and her net gain in customers left a lot to be desired.

What is one of the biggest ways to build trust and to keep customers? Do what you say you will do.

Rate Yourself

Rate Your Level of Agreement:
3 = Strongly Agree, 2 = Agree, 1 = Do Not Agree

1. I'm very clear with customers and co-workers about what I am going to do next.
   Rating: _____

2. When I tell a client I will do something, I do it or tell them why I'm having to do something different.
   Rating: _____

3. If what I'm going to do takes longer than what I noted to the customer, I'm good at following-up with the customer to reset their expectations.
   Rating: _____

4. If I handoff client responsibilities to others, I effectively follow-up with the co-worker and/or the customer to ensure satisfaction.
   Rating: _____

Total Chapter Score: _____

Record your Total Score in the "Calculate Your Greatness" table at the end of this Section.

Questions to Consider — Write Responses Below

Do you do what you said that you would do?

Do you touch base with co-workers to ensure they're progressing in helping your customer?

Do you check back with the customer to make sure they were satisfied with the resolution to the problem?

Do you waste your own time?

People Great at Customer Service...
Are Structured for Efficiency – E-mail Management

Responsiveness is not really an attitude. Where attitude comes in with responsiveness is that you have to WANT to respond to be responsive, because responsiveness requires action. If the first step in being responsive is to WANT to do it, the second step is structuring yourself to do it.

One key to being able to respond in a timely manner is to be organized enough to find things quickly. That's especially true with e-mails. Some employees get twenty e-mails a day while others get well over two hundred. With the response times that the typical customer expects, the employees need to prioritize and quickly address those communications in a timely and effective manner.

The more structured an employee is in his or her message management, the better positioned he or she is for timely communication.

Illustrating the point...
Xavier was thoroughly enjoying the customer service training, but when the content started focusing on e-mail management, he started to disagree with the training philosophy. You see, Xavier's philosophy on e-mail management was to keep all e-mails he received in his Inbox. That way, Xavier always knew where the e-mails were located. He could sort by columns and find the e-mails readily. That was his philosophy, it was simple, and he felt like it was effective for him.

But the instructor had a different take; the instructor was talking about using folders, about auto-routing e-mails into folders, about how to prioritize different messages, and about the need to segment those messages to receive the desired response level. The result was that Xavier and the instructor had an interesting dialogue during the training which essentially went like this:

- Xavier: I prefer just to keep all my e-mails in the Inbox.
- Instructor: Do you mean you don't have any folders besides the Inbox folder that you utilize?
- Xavier: Correct. That way, I always know where the messages are.
- Instructor: Interesting...do you mind if I ask you a couple questions?
- Xavier: Don't mind at all; go right ahead.
- Instructor: How many e-mails do you have right now in your Inbox?
- Xavier: Oh, probably two or three thousand. I clean out anything older than three months old unless it is really really important.
- Instructor: So if you keep the important ones that are more than two or three months old, then you must not automatically archive your e-mails. Is that correct?
- Xavier: That's correct.
- Instructor: Well if that's the case, then I imagine that you have to manually go through your e-mails every once in a while to clean out the old ones that you don't want and keep the old ones you do?

- Xavier: Right.
- Instructor: How long does that take?
- Xavier: It only takes me about thirty minutes a week.
- Instructor: Okay. How long does it take you to find an e-mail if say, Sammy over here asks about a project that he worked on a month ago?
- Xavier: It will take about a minute at the most, because I will sort by e-mails sent TO Sammy or e-mails sent FROM Sammy, and I would look through all those e-mails until I found the one relating to the project.
- Instructor: Good. Now what if it wasn't from Sammy or to Sammy. What would you do then?
- Xavier: {He pauses.} I guess that I would sort by Subject and hope that I found it.
- Instructor: How long would that take?
- Xavier: Probably not too long; I should be able to track down almost any e-mail in there in five or ten minutes.
- Instructor: One last question. What if you had to find all the e-mails relating to a particular client, which can either be internal or client-driven e-mails, and you had to route all of them to Sammy? What would you do then?
- Xavier: That's a toughie. Because they could be scattered throughout the three-plus months of e-mails under a lot of subjects, under a lot of names, and I would have to send them individually. If it's a typical client, I probably have forty to fifty different messages, so that could take me a good forty-five minutes to an hour.

- Instructor: Xavier, I'm not going to tell you how to do this, but if you want to save yourself half an hour a week, one minute every time you're asked about an e-mail that comes from a particular person or to a particular person, five to ten minutes every time you need to find an e-mail and you need to rely on the topic, and save you that full hour if you have to find a series of e-mails relating to a particular topic, then you need to rethink your e-mail management strategy. If you asked me to forward all the information I have on any project or any client, I could find and forward that information in less than fifteen seconds. And that's because of how I structure my e-mail management. It's because of the folders I use. It's because of how I use flags as well. It's because of the fields I use. So if you want to be judged as being responsive, if you want to be able to send Sammy those files in fifteen seconds instead of an hour, and if you want to save yourself time every day, consider managing your e-mails more efficiently.

There are a lot of different ways to save yourself time and to appear more responsive in front of a co-worker or customer. Utilize one simple tool – e-mail folder management.

Rate Yourself

Rate Your Level of Agreement:
3 = Strongly Agree, 2 = Agree, 1 = Do Not Agree

1. I auto-route e-mails to appropriate folders whenever possible so that those e-mails can be given the appropriate priority and reviewed at the appropriate time - either immediately or much later.
Rating: _____

2. I utilize a folder strategy that enables me to quickly find and relay information.
Rating: _____

3. I auto-archive e-mails so that older e-mails do not get unnecessarily mixed in with newer e-mails.
Rating: _____

4. I utilize fields in such a way to quickly be able to sort within a folder and find the specific communication that I need to locate.
Rating: _____

Total Chapter Score: _____

Record your Total Score in the "Calculate Your Greatness" table at the end of this Section.

Questions to Consider – Write Responses Below

Do you understand the relationship between being organized and being the best you can be at customer service?

Are you organized enough in how you manage e-mails to be responsive?

How could you become more organized in your e-mail management?

I need a quick response.

People Great at Customer Service…
Are Structured for Efficiency - Telephone Management

Individuals who are great at customer service also realize that being responsive to telephone communications requires you to be organized in how you handle those communications.

If you don't give callers an idea of your response time on your voicemail greeting, they'll set their own expectation. That expectation is often tough to meet and always unknown. If you have ten messages from ten different people, you will have to meet ten different expectations.

To be more responsive to voice mails, you should leave a standard timeframe for your return call on your voice mail greeting, along with an alternative contact if the caller does not hear back within that response time. If you'll be out of the office for an extended period, leave backup contact information. If you receive voice mails, transcribe them onto a log or onto your To Do list. They're too easily forgotten if they're simply saved on the system.

Illustrating the point...
We conducted customer service training for a client, focusing one of the modules on responsiveness. "How can you create an impression on customers that you're responsive?" we asked. The group brainstormed and came up with the following:

- **Ensuring That You Respond in a Timely Manner**. Schedule time every day to work through messages. Set a goal so you'll know by when – at the latest – you'll *respond* to all messages (even if you cannot *resolve* them within that timeframe).

- **Managing Voice Mail Messages Effectively.** Keep special logs of voice mails to ensure that they're tracked and addressed. Send e-mails to the caller when possible to acknowledge receipt of the message and to set expectations for follow-up.
- **Prioritizing Management of Messages/Responses.** Act on the urgent, important messages first. Categorize others by call type or caller type.
- **Keeping Down Backlogs.** Act on messages immediately upon receipt if at all possible, in order to keep your To Do list manageable. Have a goal for the maximum number of messages you have which must be returned.

If you want to be a responsive individual, you need to have an organized approach to managing telephone communications.

Rate Yourself

Rate Your Level of Agreement:
3 = Strongly Agree, 2 = Agree, 1 = Do Not Agree

1. I have a personal goal for the latest time after the message was left that I'll respond to the caller.
   Rating: _____

2. I acknowledge receipt of messages within that timeframe even if I cannot address the message that quickly.
   Rating: _____

3. I act on the most urgent and important first.
   Rating: _____

4. I ensure that my number of messages to address stays under a predetermined number at any point in time.
   Rating: _____

Total Chapter Score: _____

Record your Total Score in the "Calculate Your Greatness" table at the end of this Section.

Questions to Consider – Write Responses Below

Are you organized enough in how you manage your telephone messages to be responsive?

How could you become more organized in your telephone message management?

Do it right the first time.

People Great at Customer Service...
Provide Quality the First Time

You often hear the term "first call resolution" in call centers. Essentially, what you want is for the first person who receives the request or the issue to handle it. When it comes to any aspect of customer service, that same rule applies the vast majority of the time.

You also want to have high quality attitude, skills, and knowledge. If those attributes are non-existent, then you could find your time consumed with irate or upset customer conversations.

You want the process to be simple, timely, and effective right off the bat. You don't want to have to backtrack and redo something because the process caused issues.

You want the actual product or service to work well from the start; if it doesn't, you'll have to spend time dealing with duplicate complaints along with a lot of backend work just trying to salvage dollars and customer goodwill.

Individuals who are great at customer service need to be great in service recovery, but they first need to excel at doing things right the first time.

Illustrating the point...
I'm sure you've heard the expression "measure twice, cut once." Well imagine being a homeowner whose contractors repeatedly measured once, cut wrong, measured again, cut wrong, and measured again.

That's what happened to Ron. He wanted new carpeting for the first floor of his home, so he contracted with a carpet provider. The company came in, measured, cut the carpet at their warehouse, brought it out to the home, began to install it, and realized that they didn't have enough.

The contractors measured how much more was needed, cut the carpet at their warehouse, brought it out to the home, began to install it, and realized that they *still* didn't have enough.

Once again they measured how much more was needed, cut the carpet at their warehouse, brought it out to the home, installed it, and finally had enough to complete the job.

This was a waste of company time, money, labor, and a customer's patience and goodwill.

Wanting to complete the update of the first floor of the home, the same homeowner decided to get new blinds for the windows. The blinds he needed were of a non-standard size and were rectangular in shape. Ron contracted with a company to make custom-sized blinds for the home. The company representative went to the house, measured, went to the factory to have the blinds made, and brought them to the home to install. The measurements this time were perfect except for one thing...the dimensions were reversed. Instead of being 28 inches wide by 18 inches high, they were 28 inches *high* by 18 inches *wide*.

The company took the blinds back to the factory, made new ones, and brought them to the home for installation.

These companies had some positive characteristics in common. They were good at selling. They had a good product.

But they also had some bad things in common. They didn't have effective processes for gathering customer specifications and needs accurately. They didn't have effective quality assurance processes in place to make sure that the work was delivered right the first time. And they wasted time, money, and a customer's goodwill.

Many customer complaints can be avoided if the company simply takes the time upfront to gather the information and *confirm that it is correct.*

Whether you're taking measurements on carpet or you're gathering information such as demographics and customer preferences during a sale, remember to "measure twice and cut once."

Rate Yourself

Rate Your Level of Agreement:
3 = Strongly Agree, 2 = Agree, 1 = Do Not Agree

1. If others want something done right, I would be one of the first people they'd consider asking to get it done.
   Rating: _____

2. I rarely have to do rework on something I had intended to be a finished product or action.
   Rating: _____

3. It is rare for me to produce something or convey information with errors.
   Rating: _____

4. It is rare for me to produce something or convey information which is incomplete.
   Rating: _____

Total Chapter Score: _____

Record your Total Score in the "Calculate Your Greatness" table at the end of this Section.

Questions to Consider – Write Responses Below

Do you care deeply about doing things right the first time?

Do you get frustrated if you find out something you produced or shared has errors or requires rework?

Do you fully complete your work to the point that you don't miss key items to share or produce?

How can you approach your work differently so that things truly are done right the first time?

Your fault?

People Great at Customer Service...
Rarely Cause Issues

Individuals who are great at customer service rarely cause the problems or issues that they have to address. That's not to say that they won't have to deal with any issues, but there rarely arises a situation where the individual who caused the problem is great at customer service.

But that does happen. The goal, as stated earlier, is to try to do things right the first time, try to convey the appropriate attitude the first time, try to be inquisitive enough to address and understand the right need in the right way the first time.

Individuals who are great at customer service are focused on what they say, how they say it, how easy they make it for their customers to do business, and whether or not they are delivering a quality product or service. And employees who are great at customer service realize that all this is done with the understanding that they must know as precisely as possible what the customer needs before acting on that need.

Illustrating the point...
Barbara was new to her role with the organization. She had never been a customer service representative in a call center before, but she was hired because of her attitude. She wanted to learn, enjoyed working with people, and could carry on a conversation with a wall.

After going through her training on the computer and phone systems, she began to work in the live environment.

Day after day she took the calls from the customers, answering their questions and handling their complaints. As her supervisor monitored her production on the phone, he noticed an alarming statistic. Her average call length was about thirty seconds longer than the organization's target.

The supervisor needed to know why this was happening. He knew that she was a good conversationalist based on their employee meetings and her initial interviews with the company. Maybe she was talking way too much.

So he began auditing her calls, listening in for long periods of time during the day. Suddenly, several things became obvious. First, she surely was not a big talker. She had a friendly tone when she did talk, but she was actually quite quiet. Then the supervisor noted when she did talk that she would either affirm something the customer was saying or she'd ask a question.

Then he realized that she was resolving the issue herself, or getting the most appropriate answer herself to the question on that one call. There would be no need to transfer that customer, or for the customer to call back on that topic again. She didn't *cause* problems; she *solved* problems.

This was First Call Resolution at its best.

Barbara's "secret" was being a great listener. The customers loved talking with her, they got their items addressed, and they felt that someone cared about them. At the same time, she didn't talk too much, and she addressed their topics on the spot. There would be no repeat calls on the same topics from Barbara's customers.

The supervisor was so pleased with what he found that he redesigned the company's call management procedures to focus on effective listening techniques. He focused on owning the customer's satisfaction. And he focused on using effective questioning techniques to resolve issues on the first call.

The volume of calls dropped because issues got resolved, customer satisfaction soared, and employee morale grew. All because they learned how to listen.

Listen to your customers and your co-workers to serve them better.

Rate Yourself

Rate Your Level of Agreement:
3 = Strongly Agree, 2 = Agree, 1 = Do Not Agree

1. I listen to and confirm customer needs well.
   Rating: _____

2. I am very effective at specifically addressing the need the customer identified.
   Rating: _____

3. I try to make the process of working with me and my company easy on the customer.
   Rating: _____

4. I am always aware of how I'm interacting with customers to make sure there's nothing in what I say or how I say it that could create an issue.
   Rating: _____

Total Chapter Score: _____

Record your Total Score in the "Calculate Your Greatness" table at the end of this Section.

Questions to Consider – Write Responses Below

Do you make sure you have a clear understanding of what needs to be done before doing it?

Do you rarely find that something you've said or done was the cause of friction or an issue?

What can you do more effectively so that you are almost never the cause of any issue?

Are you a Mr. (or Ms.) Fix-it?

People Great at Customer Service…
Effectively Resolve Issues

If you are great at customer service, that does not mean that you're perfect at customer service. That does not mean that you work in a perfect organization with perfect processes, policies, systems, and co-workers. In other words, everybody has to deal with issues.

Individuals who are great at customer service care about resolving issues quickly. There have been studies done that show your ability to retain a customer is directly related to how quickly and effectively you resolve their problems.

Individuals who are great at customer service understand the true impact that they have when a customer has a complaint. At that moment of truth, the employee has the potential to save a relationship, to change an organization's reputation, and to have a huge long-term financial impact on the business.

Whereas those outcomes are positive, individuals who are not great at customer service have the same potential to break a relationship, to tarnish the organization's reputation, and to convert what could be a large lifetime value of a customer into a one-time transactional value.

Illustrating the point…
They didn't "get it."

An article published by Bloomberg News noted how one computer manufacturer received four calls from a 74-year-old customer who had just bought a new desktop computer.

The calls were made because the computer's operating system didn't work. Those four calls left him on hold for 363 minutes total – an average hold time of 91 minutes per call. He then wrote a letter to the manufacturer with his complaint; the letter was returned as undeliverable.

When asked if he'd ever buy a computer from that company again, his response was "no, ma'am." That 74-year-old customer had since warned six friends against buying a computer from that manufacturer.

One has to wonder if that customer had to wait 91 minutes to *buy* the computer in the first place. One also has to wonder if this company values word-of-mouth and repeat business.

Why is this anecdote important from a business perspective? Well over the past six years, the company's stock has dropped 61%, down 24% in the most recent year alone. Part of how they want to turn around company performance is to invest $150 million in customer service. That investment in customer service coincides with a plan to reduce $3 billion in costs elsewhere. In other words, the share of the budget pie that is going to customer service will increase significantly.

Responsiveness impacts the bottom line. Word-of-mouth impacts the bottom line. Issue resolution impacts the bottom line. Customer service impacts the bottom line.

Maybe the results of poor customer service aren't as readily apparent as a contract on a new sale, but – like a virus – at some point poor customer service will make your Income Statement sick.

Make sure your company gets the link between service and business success.

Make sure you are fixing issues before those dissatisfied customers break the company.

Rate Yourself

Rate Your Level of Agreement:
3 = Strongly Agree, 2 = Agree, 1 = Do Not Agree

1. When dealing with an issue, I attempt to quickly find a resolution.
   Rating: _____

2. I work hard to make sure the resolution will balance the customer's needs and the organizational goals.
   Rating: _____

3. I fully understand how issue resolution impacts retention and future business, which impacts organizational success.
   Rating: _____

4. I am confident about how to resolve issues or about how to find others who can quickly resolve them.
   Rating: _____

Total Chapter Score: _____

Record your Total Score in the "Calculate Your Greatness" table at the end of this Section.

Questions to Consider – Write Responses Below

Are you effective at taking an issue and moving it forward to resolution?

Are you effective at getting buy-in to your solutions?

Do you effectively facilitate discussions with others to help them develop their own solutions?

How could you be more solution-oriented (as opposed to blame-oriented) when issues arise?

You don't have to be Shakespeare, but...

People Great at Customer Service...
Communicate Well in Writing

People who are great at customer service know how to write. Communication is not just the words you say or your body language or tone of voice; it also includes written communication.

When writing, you should personalize the communications and write them in a professional, business letter format. Particularly for e-mails, you want the reader to understand your key points in a very quick and concise manner. You want to provide "meat" in the *Subject Header* as well as in the *Body* of the e-mail.

Consider the tone of the wording. Written documents don't have a tone of voice to appropriately convey emotion, so word choice is particularly important.

You should *always* spell-check before sending. An intelligent person can look dumb, impatient, rude, uncaring, or just plain incompetent when he or she sends an e-mail riddled with spelling or grammatical errors.

Illustrating the point...
You've probably heard the expression "the right hand doesn't know what the left hand is doing." To a small business owner, this analogy applied to a product issue.

Jeff was printing off multiple copies of a final report with his color laser printer. It was mid-afternoon, and the report was due for presentation in a meeting first thing the next morning. Jeff noticed that the printer had stopped printing, and it needed a new magenta (basically pink) print cartridge. He had one available, so he put it in the printer. Immediately the pages started printing out pink. Every single page was pink!

Jeff started freaking out. Was the printer damaged? Was there any way that this project could be printed and put together by his meeting in the morning? Why was this happening?!

Jeff stopped the printing and drove to the local office supply store. He bought another magenta printer cartridge and went back to the office and inserted a new cartridge. Luckily, after about twenty sheets printed, the pages began to look normal again.

The next day, after his morning presentation, Jeff called his account representative with the online vendor from whom he had purchased the cartridge. The representative apologized profusely, and even though he noted that the damaged cartridge was more than thirty days old – the company "grace period" for returns – he still okayed its return. The representative explained to Jeff how to return the cartridge, and Jeff felt satisfied.

A couple hours later, Jeff received an e-mail. The following was all of the information included in the e-mail:

SUBJECT: *Inv# 54592ABC case#30-2951ABC*

BODY: *COMPANY has a 30 day return policy and this inv# is well over the time frame of returns. We are not able to return this order. Thank you.*

Jeff was furious! Not only did the e-mail contradict what the account representative had told him, but he was upset that he would not be able to return a cartridge that almost damaged his printer and caused the print job not to work.

What's more than that was that it was a horribly constructed e-mail. The e-mail address from which it came was some kind of a cryptic set of letters, and the only reason why Jeff knew that it was not spam was that the URL was that of his online office supply vendor.

The subject heading made no sense and offered no helpful information. The e-mail seemed very cold and harsh. It seemed like a negative, auto-generated e-mail with no personalized greeting, no statement of empathy or understanding about the customer's frustration, and no name or contact information at the end. Not only did it contradict what the account representative had said, but it also was harsh, negative, cold, and unclear.

You can say the same thing in writing in two different ways and come across dramatically differently. This is an example of how the tone of the e-mail could have been positively impacted by better business writing skills.

You need to think of an e-mail as a business letter, not a text message, not a live chat, not a two-way telephone conversation. The reason is that e-mail is a one-way communication, and because there is no body language to see or voice to hear, the words have to convey the right tone.

To convey the right tone there needs to be personalization at the start and at the end. There need to be statements of empathy or understanding when you're telling information the customer may not want to hear. There need to be statements of appreciation or thanks included when communicating with the customer. And there need to be subject headings that have meaning and tell a story about what the e-mail is about or what follow-up is requested.

Don't let personal laziness or a misunderstanding of what type of communication e-mail is to keep you from making a good impression on your customer or your co-worker.

Rate Yourself

Rate Your Level of Agreement:
3 = Strongly Agree, 2 = Agree, 1 = Do Not Agree

1. I use personalized greetings and closings in e-mails to set a professional and cordial tone.
   Rating: _____

2. I include descriptive information in the Subject field so the recipient has a clear understanding of the message topic.
   Rating: _____

3. I make a conscious effort to convey the appropriate tone in what I say when I communicate via e-mail.
   Rating: _____

4. I always proof and spell-check my e-mails before sending.
   Rating: _____

Total Chapter Score: _____

Record your Total Score in the "Calculate Your Greatness" table at the end of this Section.

Questions to Consider – Write Responses Below

Do you consider the quality of your writing to be professional? Would others agree?

Are you clear and specific in what you convey?

Do you convey information in as simple a way as possible – avoiding acronyms and technical jargon when the other person is clearly not familiar with these terms?

Do you convey information as concisely as possible?

How can you write in such a way that the reader has an even better chance of quickly understanding your point?

Why are we here?

People Great at Customer Service...
Are Outcomes-Oriented

You could have the best attitude in the world, you could have the best processes known to man, and you could have seemingly excellent products and services. However, what matters is the customer's perception of that service's outcome. Notice how we did not say that the outcome itself is what matters. The customer's opinion is based on their perception of the outcome, not necessarily the reality of that outcome.

There is almost always a difference between expectations and reality, but there are also differences between perception and reality at times.

Individuals who are great at customer service are focused on providing the outcome that the customer wants, whether the customer wants a product provided in a timely manner, or a service provided easily, or information being provided accurately.

Customers define companies as being great at customer service if the customer perceives that the outcome was great. The customer has to feel and understand the value of that outcome. Individuals who are great at customer service focus on client outcomes.

Illustrating the point...
We were working with a healthcare system several years ago which had a group of very dissatisfied physicians working in the physician clinics. One of the reasons for this dissatisfaction

was that the physicians would try to schedule an outpatient procedure, such as a radiology exam, but the lead time for such non-urgent exams was typically several weeks. The physicians were very upset that it took so long for their patients to get some of these common procedures done.

So what did the hospital do? They launched a task force to totally redesign the scheduling processes. They altered their staffing. They changed how the procedures were managed, how the timeslots were set, and how the scheduling process flowed. They made dramatic improvements, reducing the lead time from many weeks to less than 10 days.

The hospital surveyed the physicians again about their satisfaction with the scheduling process, expecting to get rave reviews from doctors. But instead, the results came back negative. The physicians were upset, they were irate, they were throwing a fit over the length of time it took to schedule their patients into these procedures.

Why in the world were the physicians so upset?

Their reality had changed for the better. The lead time had been reduced dramatically. But as the physicians were completing the surveys, they were still thinking about the bad situations that their patients had run into 6, 9, or 12 months earlier. So even though the hospital had changed the outcomes, they had failed to change the end customers' perception of the outcome. Even though the scheduling staff at the physician clinics knew that the performance had been improved, that knowledge was not really there for the physicians as well.

So the hospital learned that they not only needed to improve the process, but they needed to communicate that improvement to their customers as well. Because even though the reality may be better, perception may not be any better at all.

The next time you're making an improvement, don't assume that everyone will see and applaud your efforts. Make sure you're communicating that improvement to impact perception as well as reality.

Rate Yourself

Rate Your Level of Agreement:
3 = Strongly Agree, 2 = Agree, 1 = Do Not Agree

1. I am as much focused on the goal or outcome I am trying to achieve as I am the task I'm doing to achieve the goal.
   Rating: _____

2. I not only complete work, but I communicate back to the stakeholders that the work was completed.
   Rating: _____

3. When I communicate back to stakeholders about work being completed, I also communicate the impact or benefit of that action, whenever possible.
   Rating: _____

4. When making improvements, I execute communication plans that ensure others are aware of the progress and impact of the improvements being made.
   Rating: _____

Total Chapter Score: _____

Record your Total Score in the "Calculate Your Greatness" table at the end of this Section.

Questions to Consider – Write Responses Below

When you are working on a task, activity, or project, do you maintain a clear vision of *why* you're doing it?

Do you communicate status updates with customers and co-workers as you work on activities or projects?

Do you communicate to customers and other stakeholders that you have completed the work?

If so, when you communicate to customers and other stakeholders about completed work, do you also tell them the outcome of the work?

How can you become more focused on the benefits of what you say and do rather than the task or the process you're going through?

Calculate Your Greatness – Are You Great When the Customer's Not in Front of You?

Enter your total score from the chapter noted below in the spaces provided to the right.

Find the common ground.   Total Chapter Score: _____

To be or not to be...in touch.   Total Chapter Score: _____

Don't drop the ball.   Total Chapter Score: _____

Do you waste your own time?   Total Chapter Score: _____

I need a quick response.   Total Chapter Score: _____

Do it right the first time.   Total Chapter Score: _____

Your fault?   Total Chapter Score: _____

Are you a Mr. (or Ms.) Fix-it?   Total Chapter Score: _____

You don't have to be Shakespeare, but...   Total Chapter Score: _____

Why are we here?   Total Chapter Score: _____

Add Total Chapter Scores to Get Your Total Section Score: _____

Interpreting Your Scores...

    111-120 - You are GREAT even when you're not in front of a customer!

101-110 - You have many of the key qualities required to be great even when you're not in front of a customer.

    Under 101 - There's work to be done.

Needing to improve? Look back to the chapters where you scored lowest and focus on the tips and questions. You can also get a more personal detailed assessment with recommendations at <u>www.amigreatat.com</u>.

Calculate Your Greatness

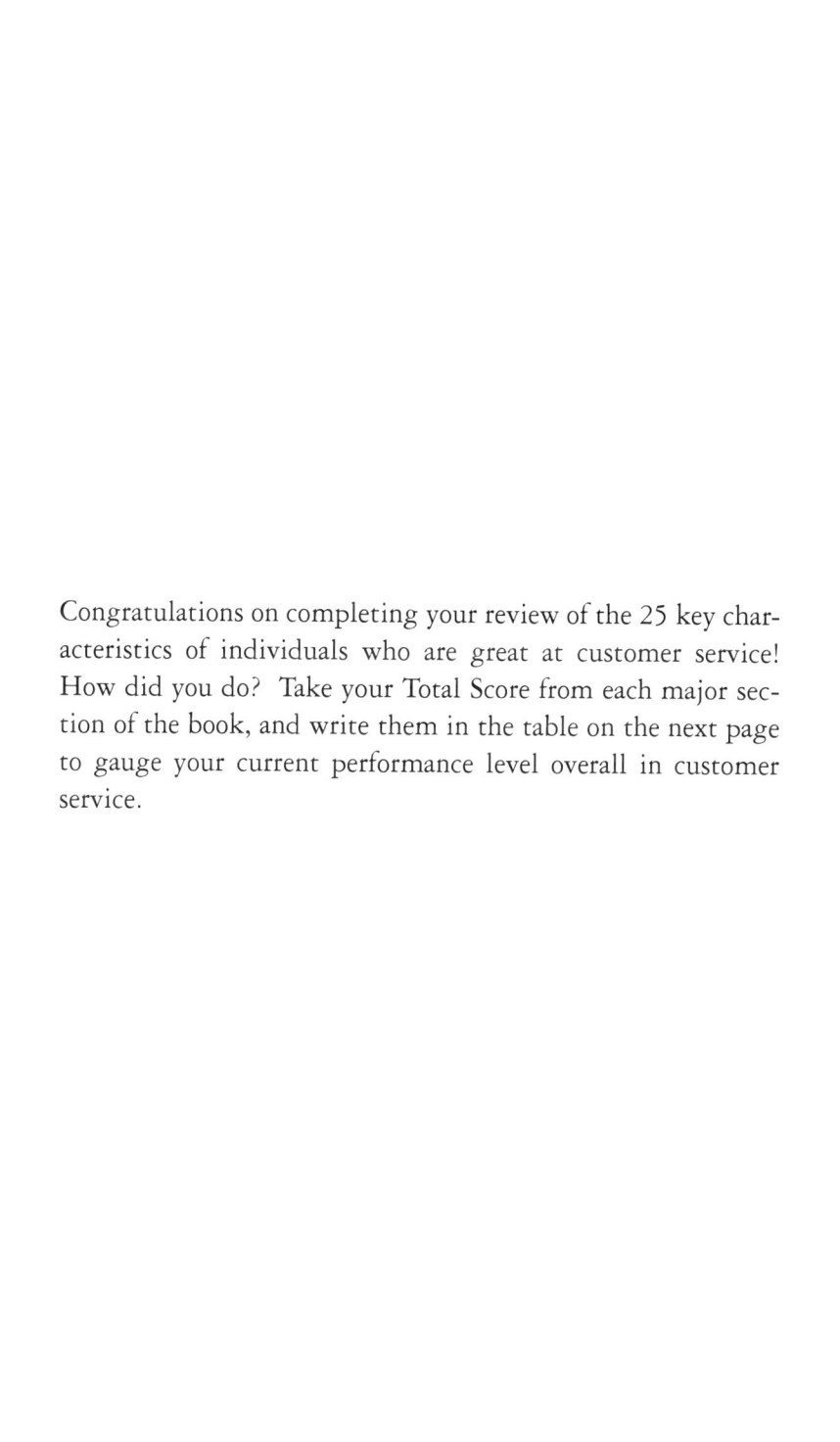

Congratulations on completing your review of the 25 key characteristics of individuals who are great at customer service! How did you do? Take your Total Score from each major section of the book, and write them in the table on the next page to gauge your current performance level overall in customer service.

Calculate Your Greatness – Overall

Enter your total score from each Section noted below in the spaces provided to the right.

Is Your Attitude Great?　　　　　　Your Section Score: _____

*Are You Great When You're In
Front of the Customer?*　　　　　　Your Section Score: _____

*Are You Great When the Customer's
Not in Front of You?*　　　　　　　Your Section Score: _____

**Add Total Section Scores to Get Your Grand
　　　　　　　　　　　　　　　　Total Score:** _____

Interpreting Your Scores…

　　277-300 - You are truly GREAT at customer service!

　　258-276 - You have many of the key qualities required to be great at customer service.

　　Under 258 - There's work to be done.

*You can also get a more personal detailed assessment with recommendations at www.am**i**great**at**.com.*

Remember that People Great at Customer Service…

- Have a Positive Orientation
- Hone Their Knowledge/Skills
- Convey Patience
- Have a Kaizen Mindset
- Are Focused on the Other Person
- Empathize with the Customer
- Have a Learning Orientation
- View Co-workers as Customers
- Are Willing to Share Bad News
- Choose Their Words Effectively
- Are Effective Non-Verbal Communicators
- Use Effective Call Handling Techniques
- Converse Well
- Defuse the Upset/Irate Customer
- Effectively Set and Manage Expectations
- Know How to Build Relationships
- Are Responsive
- Follow-Up and Follow-Through
- Are Structured for Efficiency – E-mail Management
- Are Structured for Efficiency – Telephone Management
- Provide Quality the First Time
- Rarely Cause Issues
- Effectively Resolve Issues
- Communicate Well in Writing
- Are Outcomes-Oriented

Now ask yourself, "Am I GREAT at Customer Service?"

About the Author

Ed Gagnon is a business owner, customer retention strategist, customer service consultant, researcher, trainer, writer, and speaker.

As President of Charlotte, NC-based Customer Service Solutions, Inc., a customer service and retention consulting, research, and training firm founded in 1998, Ed has helped hundreds of clients improve their bottom line by improving their customer service.

Ed uses his 20+ years of consulting experience to help CSS clients through Fast-Track Culture Assessments, Client Retention and Growth Strategy development, service process redesign, customer service training, and research services such as perceptions surveys and mystery shopping.

Ed has been interviewed on customer service by such publications as the New York Times, Kiplinger Business Forecasts, The Christian Science Monitor, and Human Resource Executive. Ed has also been featured on television and radio, written hundreds of articles on customer service, and he blogs on customer service on the CSS website www.cssamerica.com.

As an engaging and well-respected speaker, Ed always delivers an energetic and personalized message to his audience – whether they are executives or front-line staff – inspiring them to improve.